SHE
PROFITS

The Outrageously Simple
5-Point Entrepreneurial
Profit Plan

*Thank you for allowing me
to be a part of your journey!*

Mel McSherry

BtB
publishing

PRINT ISBN: 978-1-7357404-0-9
eBOOK ISBN: 978-1-7357404-1-6

SHE
PROFITS

CONTENTS

CHAPTER 1

THE BIG PROBLEM
WITH PLANNING

EACH YEAR, THOUSANDS OF new businesses are started, backed by women entrepreneurs who dream to become successful and build something great. But did you know that since 2007,[1] the number of female-owned businesses has catapulted to over five times the national average? Furthermore, you can do specific things (such as following my 5 Step plan) to keep yourself and your business out of the 20% category of small businesses that go under in the first year or the 50% that don't make it to five years.

The biggest reason for failure is lack of planning, or more to the point, planning with a lack of prioritization. You see, every single one of us has unlimited potential when it comes to the success we want to create within our businesses. However, so many of us don't even get close because we get lost in everything we THINK we need to do to create the success that we want.

Not only what we need to do but also in whom we need to be. But guess what, YOU ARE PERFECT! You have everything inside you to answer the call of your soul. You just need to find it and then create a prioritized plan of action that will help you create the business, money, and the life you want.

Whether you are a natural "planner" or not, this book will help you identify what you want, tame the time that you have, and create a prioritized plan of action that is customized to

---

1   Francis, Stacy. "11 Tips for 11 Million Women - How Female Entrepreneurs Can Beat the Odds." CNBC. October 21, 2019. https://www.cnbc.com/2019/10/21/how-todays-11-million-female-entrepreneurs-can-beat-the-odds.html

your goals, your time, and your energy. As a result, EVERY DAY you can create success in your business.

I have shared this system to thousands of women, just like you, who are overwhelmed and exhausted by everything you think you need to do to be successful through my workshops, 1:1 coaching, and social media posts. Some have shared that this "system" has helped create the business, the money and the life they want, *and* the confidence to know they have full say on how they spend their time, as soon as they start applying it! Others have messaged me letting me know they had doubled their monthly income, on top of, still having a life!

How fucking awesome is that?!

How would you like to be profitable mentally, emotionally, and financially, every day?

This book is going to show you how outrageously simple it is.

"Well, Mel, if it's so simple, why isn't everyone doing it?"

Because it's not easy. It's not easy for women to put themselves and their business at the top of the list—this woman included. Instead, we exhaust, overextend ourselves, and wish for more time in the day.

Raise your hand if that is you because that was definitely me back in 2015.

MY STORY

That's exactly where I was in 2015. I was building two different businesses at the time, I was also a part-time virtual administrator for an IT company in Dallas, I had a four-year-old son running around who was just recognized for being on the autism spectrum AND I was in the beginning stages of my divorce…Needless to say, my plate was just a little full.

Now, when I say I was building different businesses, that's actually a little bit of a lie because, honestly, I was building nothing more than a lot of stress, debt, and a really bad attitude. Why was that? Because I was putting everybody else's needs before my own.

I was putting my clients' needs first because I wanted them to be successful. I put my son's needs first, because well, I just wanted to keep him alive as well as really wrap my head around how his life will be. We know kids don't show up in the delivery room with a detailed set of instructions, so on top of still getting a handle on this whole mom thing, I am now overwhelmed with all this new information. While I love being his mom, it's a continual learning process for me as to how to do that to the best of my ability while serving his highest good.

With all of that going on, I was doing absolutely nothing for myself. I was going to bed every single night so exhausted, wondering how I could possibly be so busy throughout each and every day, yet I was seeing nothing coming back to me.

Especially nothing that was profitable—mentally, emotionally, OR financially.

Mine had become a revolving door existence of "same shit, different day." I was sick of it but hadn't a clue as to how to get off of the hamster wheel. Until...

My OHF! Moment

Fast forward to one day, when I took one small step that changed the entire trajectory of my business and myself. It's so crazy how one small step or one small change in your daily routine can create such an amazing snowball effect.

And that day went like this:

My IT client messaged me after I had just perfectly scheduled out my day and had forty-five minutes to devote entirely to my own two businesses. It doesn't seem like a lot, but it was more than I typically had from day-to-day. As I was ready to start my day, my Google Hangouts notification went off and revealed a question from my IT client that made me cringe. And that question was, "Can you do me a favor?"

Of course, out loud to my computer screen I yelled, "NO!" but then I took a deep breath and simply replied, "What's up?" He then told me how he needed this massive report by the end of the day for a project he was pitching at the end of the month.

Now, I knew with every fiber of my being that this actually did not need to be done that day. In fact, I knew I could get it done by the end of the next day and we would still be about two weeks ahead of time to pitch this project.

We always know things like that right?

But, instead of telling him right away what I knew, telling him what I need and asking for what I want, I started playing an internal game of Tetris. That was my knee-jerk go-to move, to start rearranging my schedule completely around his request.

I was thinking, "Okay, I could skip lunch. I could sleep three hours instead of four. I've done it before, I can do it again, and I can find time for myself tomorrow." Just juggling this all mentally, I could feel the inevitable exhaustion creeping in. I was setting myself up for yet another "Groundhog Day"—same old, same old.

Sound familiar?

But for whatever reason, after going through all of these mental gymnastics, I had this major "Oh holy fuck" moment. It was just this small act of realizing that if I continuously rearrange my priorities to meet somebody else's request I'm always going to feel this way. And the only way that I'm going to get this trajectory to stop is if I stop it; no one is going to magically discover how stressed I am, then swoop in and save me. To quote my old karate master, "If it has to be, it's up to me."

If I truly recognize who I am, what I want, and ask for what I need accordingly, based upon my priorities and my time, I will have established the boundaries I have been craving.

P.S. This beautiful and game-changing epiphany was completely internal.

Externally, I began writing him back a massively involved, overly apologetic reason of why I'm not going to get this done today. Within the context of that note, I found myself basically throwing everybody under the bus. "Oh, I can't do that today because I've got my son…" and blah, blah, blah. Trying to blame it on anyone and everyone else. Here I was constructing this detailed apology foisting the reason for it off on others.

But even as I wrote it, it didn't ring true. It was not authentic and was not the reason. The reason was that I knew the report could easily be done by the end of the day tomorrow and that we would still be ahead of schedule.

So I reread that bullshit apology one more time and then deleted the whole thing.

Instead of sending that, as I would have automatically done up until that day, I replaced it with this: "I'm all booked up today. I can have it for you by the end-of-day tomorrow, which will still give you two weeks ahead of the deadline to pitch the project. If you have any questions, let me know." And I hit send.

And then I wanted to throw up.

Because I thought I "knew" exactly how he was going to react. I just knew that he was going to think that I was incapable of my job, that I was stupid, he was going to be so mad, he was going to fire me, etc., etc., etc.

We have these worst-case scenario conversations that go on in our heads all the time. We create such huge monsters in our imagination about how others may react to us. Like that monster under the bed when we were kids. The longer we fixated on it, the bigger it seemed to us. But here's something cool about that: because we're the one that created this monster to begin with, we're also the one that can shine the light under the bed and realize it's nothing but a fear-based illusion.

So that's what I did.

Twenty-five seconds later, while this huge argument was going on in my head, the notification alarm went off again and he simply responded, "Sounds great. See you tomorrow."

I'm sorry, what now?

I was stunned!

Has it always been that simple? And the thing is, Yeah! It really is that simple.

However, we, as women, tend to make it so much harder for ourselves because we feel like that's part of the process. We feel like, in order to be successful, we have to constantly be exhausted, constantly overextended, constantly wondering where the money will come from to cover our most basic expenses. "The hustle is real"—actually, the "hustle" is bullshit.

But you say, "But look! I'm so busy every day. Isn't that a good thing?"

Yeah, you're busy, all right, but are you being profitable—mentally, emotionally OR financially?

See, up until that "OHF" moment, I was 'so busy' but I was also chronically broke and exhausted.

By simply taking that small step to make crystal clear what I wanted, tame the time that I had, and ask for what I needed, I was able to achieve things so much faster in my personal life and my professional life.

In fact, three years later, I nearly tripled my annual income, became an international speaker, spoke over seventy times (twice internationally), and became an Amazon bestselling author all while being the primary caregiver to my son.

I now go to bed every single night feeling profitable—mentally, emotionally, financially, and successful and happy. I wake up every single day excited, with a customized, simple plan of action that helps me create what I want.

Long story short?

The **OHF!** led me directly to developing my *5 Point Profit Priority Plan,* which is designed to help women business owners/entrepreneurs who are exhausted and overwhelmed by everything they *think* they need to do to be successful. This plan slashes their stress by showing them how to correctly prioritize their time, their profit avenues and themselves so they can create what they want in the time that they have!

My mission with this book is to share that plan with you. Obviously, you're reading this book because you're searching for a profit plan, right? Well, you're in the right place because this is an outrageously simple entrepreneurial profit plan. We know the numbers are dismal around entrepreneurship, especially when it relates to women's success. But I'm here to tell you it doesn't have to be that way. Oh, and FYI, a goal without a plan is just a wish.

The real problem most people have that runs them into metaphorical brick walls concerns planning. That's what I've discovered over the last decade of working with hundreds of entrepreneurs. We've all heard the old adage about how failure is a result of failing to plan, not planning to fail. Obviously, it's never the entrepreneur's or businessperson's plan to fail. You don't plan to fail; you fail to plan.

But I'm going to help you avoid falling into that trap ever again. As I said, these steps are really simple and the 5 Steps work again and again and again. They have for me and for hundreds of people that I've spoken to, worked with, and coached. You'll get it pretty quickly that I cut right to the chase and tell it like it is—and that's what makes me your raw, take no prisoners planning expert. My passion is to help phenomenal women like yourself.

Quick rundown of how this book is going to work. As I have said before, this is about creating your profit prioritized plan and putting it into ACTION.

In the next chapter, I'm going to share Step 1: Identify What You Want. I've created the book's format to include a chapter that covers each of the 5 Steps, followed by 3 Get Started Action Steps, and ending with stories that illustrate how each step works successfully. Then it's basically rinse and repeat with each chapter and Steps. Just FYI, I'm letting you know that when I share someone else's stories, I've changed names, not because they didn't fare well, but because they did. It's simply to protect their privacy and anonymity.

I'm asking that you make a commitment right now to actually DO those Action Steps, because I don't want you leaving all dressed up with nowhere to go. You've got to be ready to roll and each chapter is going to set you up for success where you learn it tonight, try it tomorrow.

Don't worry. I'm also going to include all the Action Steps in an Appendix at the end of the book as well as some bonus resources so you can pull them up any time you feel the need for a refresher.

So, are you ready to create the business, the money, and the life you want in the time you have?

Fan-fucking-tastic!

Let's move on to the next chapter.

·

CHAPTER 2

STEP #1:
IDENTIFY WHAT YOU WANT:
IT'S NOT ALWAYS WHAT YOU
THINK IT MIGHT BE

WHAT WE WILL BE covering in this chapter:

- Identify:
  - What you want in your business—not what you think you CAN achieve, but what you WANT to achieve.
  - Who can support you to get what you want?
  - Who you need to be to get what you want?
  - Who do you want to work with?

When you identify what you want, this becomes your "true north" so you know which direction you need to go, and what tools/resources you need, to create what you want. Clarity is key, just like asking for directions: you get there a lot faster when you ask where a specific address is instead of, "you know, that one house by that one tree…"

My Story

I had the privilege of being mentored by the world-renowned business coach, John C. Maxwell, and one of his quotes has been my guiding light from the day I heard it:

"Learn to say 'no' to the good, so you can say 'yes' to the best."

This was especially apparent when I said 'no' to my good marriage.

Say what?

Yep, I asked for a divorce out of a good marriage.

Let me give you a bit of background before sharing that story here. While growing up, and for the longest time, my goal was to be mediocre, to be average. My mantra was to just keep up and make do with what I have. This type of perspective shifted as my relationships did. I started molding myself into what was not already present in my life with whatever group I was part of at the moment.

Whether I had to be the funny one, the quiet one, or the mediator, I would fashion myself into whoever I needed to be in that particular group to be accepted. Even when I started my first business in the fitness industry in 2010, I did so just to make some type of contribution. I had never set sales goals for myself, I just wanted to be able to financially help out with my marriage, family, and any other obligations.

So basically, I had never strived to be anything but average. It wasn't until I started doing personal development religiously, that I began to notice that I was starting to form new beliefs. Better beliefs.

John Maxwell calls this set of actions, "lifting the lid."

I kept seeing the lid each time I was presented with a new opportunity and began to notice where I was stopping myself from growing and improving my life. I realized that a lot of stress and frustration was a result of not giving myself permission to hone in on what I wanted.

I remember that first moment when I had this realization of, *"Holy shit! I could create something that's amazing! Not only amazing, but also I could make really good money doing what I love doing because I am pretty fucking good at it!"*

That was the first glimmer of excitement and connectivity to that spark when you realize there is something *more* to you than what you have been doing—something that might challenge you but also holds the strong possibility of growing you and improving your life as well as the lives of those around you.

This realization helped me laser in on such questions as: *Where am I spending my time? Who am I spending it with? What am I actually receiving from it?* These questions then set off a light bulb moment that kept lighting up, week after week, to help me obtain that return on investment in my new focus, both mentally and emotionally. That's the point when I started growing more and more.

Now back to my marriage.

Even though I was being led to shift, my husband remained who he is, which was fine because he's fantastic. But it did come to a point where I had to sit with myself and ask the question again, "What do *I* want?" when it came to my marriage.

It was extremely difficult, and I did a ton of soul-searching as well as several therapy appointments to get the clarity I needed. I clearly remember that day I dived in and asked him for a divorce. It was heartbreaking. I cried, he cried, but it was definitely something that I now look back on and know it was the right thing to do. Because if I could say no to a good marriage and continue to build what I want, what other best things can I now say yes to?

To this day, that decision strengthened not only my relationship with myself but also my relationship with my ex-husband and his relationship with our son.

I discovered I pretty much had the strength to do anything.

That major personal moment of clarity of, "What do I want?" continues to help me decide on what's best to say yes to, and what's good to say no to. It has given me my true north direction.

Now, I'm not saying by determining what you want will mean you need a divorce, but I'm going to be honest—as soon as you start putting yourself first, relationships ARE going to change because you will no longer fit the category someone put you in—or you put yourself in—when they met you.

Don't let someone's opinion of your past self, stop you from becoming your future best self.

"What do I want?"

YOU HAVE EVERYTHING INSIDE OF YOU TO ANSWER THE CALL OF YOUR SOUL. YOU JUST HAVE TO FIND IT.

I tell my clients this all the time and what I mean by it is that you're absolutely capable of attracting everything that you want in order to create your ideal life and business. But there is a practice to finding it and **SPOILER ALERT:** It's not an instantaneous satisfaction or solution where you just ask the question and BANG! you get the answer immediately. Like everything else that is worth its weight in gold, it's a process. With consistency comes clarity.

I have found that just sitting down with yourself for a good old-fashioned talk/ self-examination can amplify that clarity so much more. You may balk about this at first, because it's hard or uncomfortable to sit down with yourself. Because when you do that, you actually have to recognize and confront some things that you have likely been trying to avoid.

For the love of God do NOT punish yourself for whatever decision you made back then, or the mindset you had. You may think this is a tired old nugget of wisdom, but I find it's still timely: "Everything happens for a reason." You have to choose to get to this point so that you can have the resources, foresight, hindsight, or whatever to now say,

"Okay, I now know what it is I don't want because I've been through all of this."

That's a really great identifier. It's so helpful to know exactly what you *don't* want, because that then makes what you *do* want so much clearer and more prevalent.

Think about when you go out on a first date (or when you used to if that's more applicable). You're usually so excited that right at the tip of your consciousness, you're thinking, "This is great, this is what I want. I'll just ignore those little red flags that are hiding in the background." But if you're tuned in to what you don't want and the red flags pop up, you can't ignore or just glaze over them. It becomes a more intensive deciding factor.

It's the same thing when you're identifying what you want in anything. You simply need to laser in and identify, "Okay, this is what I don't want. These are my non-negotiables in this situation." Finding that clarity of what you truly want just becomes a bigger presence once you've eliminated the "don't want."

Now back to what you do want.

Let's chat about comparison syndrome. Speaking from a female standpoint, when we start a new venture, we tend to compare ourselves to other successful women who seem to have the Midas touch. We lose sight of the fact that they most likely had to go through a number of attempts prior to getting what they want. Instead of identifying how we work and then customizing their processes to it, we think that we have to be exactly like them: same language, same process, same look, etc. and we will create the results they did. But that is not how this works!

You know you want that degree of success, but you still don't know how you want to create it. Many of the women I work with, especially in the first two to three months, are still trying to connect to what kind of business they even want theirs to be. One of the questions I ask them is,

"Do you actually want this to be a lifestyle or an empire?"

Those are different things, so which do you want? Do you want to create something that is just for you, or do you want to create a massive empire that will last way after you're gone? You can always change your mind, but for right now, what do you want to create with this business idea?

When I work with creatives, especially, they always have a ton of ideas, which I love. But I also love to play devil's advocate and ask them, "Okay, where in this big picture do you see this falling into place? Do you feel we need to start implementing it now to strengthen what we've already created? Or maybe this is something we can just put a pin in, strengthen the rest of these areas/issues, and then it will just naturally happen?"

Then there's that centuries' old statement that it's a woman's prerogative to change her mind. In my work, I find that many women actually feel guilty if they change their mind.

They deem it as a failure. But I'm here to remind you that it's always okay to change your mind. It's okay to say yes to something and then actually take a moment, shift, and realize,

"No, I don't want to do that." Then you can come back and say, "You know what? I'm no longer available."

Granted, that process can be difficult. I had to work a lot on that myself, but when you take into consideration the limited time that you have and you seize control of your time, that's incredibly empowering. It helps you remember that you actually do have full control, for the most part. This process brings you back to really knowing why you're spending your time there, and what that is connected to. My friend and publisher, Melissa Wilson likes to say, "I can tell the sign of a successful entrepreneur by the number of times he or she can say no."

Bestselling author and marketing coach Eric Worre is fond of saying, "You should go for no." I agree with that philosophy, because the more "no's" that you choose to give, the more space you create in your life for the big "yeses." It's a numbers game. The more things you say no to leaves you open for so many more yeses that are actually more profitable to you mentally, emotionally, and financially.

I've discovered that most women, especially when they first start working with me, say yes to everything out of fear. That fosters a lack of abundance. They say yes to everything, because it's yes to a paycheck, it's yes to exposure. When they do that, guess what happens? All of a sudden, they find themselves overextended overwhelmed and as poor as can be.

I'm talking as poor as can be on multiple levels—mentally, emotionally, and financially. It's like they've died. I want to stress here that always saying yes is not some rite of passage to becoming an entrepreneur. Hustling is not a rite of passage.

Always bring it back to center for yourself and know that it's just a matter of, "What do I want to create?" Identify that, and then your next step is to take inventory of, "What are the resources I already have that are aligned with what I want?" Then ask yourself, "How can I start utilizing my strengths to get closer to my goal and continue the journey forward?""

Always saying yes can be seductive at first. Because it makes you feel that you never let anyone down, you're always there when someone needs you. But you're just one person, with only so much energy and time, remember. So, I'm here to bust that myth and tell you that it is something you may choose to think of as "the illusion of yes." It's a big pain point to figure out, "How do I jump over that hurdle and get better at saying no to things I don't want to do?"

When you find your non-negotiable "Yeses," then every day you have something to look forward to and be excited about. That gets you going and motivates you onto the next day.

Your constant question becomes, "What do I want now?" Every time you look at your goal board or list, you see what you accomplished the month before, what worked and what didn't. When I work with somebody, my goal is to push them to do what they repeatedly said they wanted to do. They usually want my accountability on that. Without it, they keep stopping themselves from doing it. Any time that happens, then we have a moment of clarity that begs the question, "Is this really connected with what I want, or do I just think I should do this because I thought of it?"

*DAWN'S STORY

I'll use a true story to illustrate this point. A friend of mine was in Oak Park, Illinois, visiting one of the houses that Frank Lloyd Wright built and lived in. It was an absolutely beautiful cornerstone house. She and her friend saw a house for sale across the street. They decided to walk over and take a look, just out of curiosity. The backyard space was gorgeous. Turns out the woman who owned it was a graphic designer, and she actually had converted that space into a design studio. Talk about a huge she-shed!

The owner happened to be present, and as people were milling around, my friend went up to her and said, "Wow! This is so amazing. How did you ever do that? But why would you want to leave this and move?" The designer's reply was, "Well, you see, the problem is I got involved in too many things, saying yes to them. The PTA, being a classroom mom..." She went on and on. Just because she couldn't say no, she decided the best thing she could do was to abandon a home she had poured her heart and soul into and start over again someplace new.

This is a classic example of how many women, rather than face the resulting reality that their inability to say no has created, and try to understand and grow from that, they choose to run away from it. Believe me, if that's your choice, I guarantee you'll find that pattern will follow you and eventually bite you in the ass!

By not changing your behavior, you don't shift any neurology or any tendencies of habit. If you choose to run away, that's just teaching yourself and your children, if you have them, that instead of facing things, learning to say no and how to change your mind, that you're willing to completely uproot everything that you've worked so hard to build. When we make such a decision, it's definitely going to reinforce that negative pattern and be staring you in the face, once again, not too far down the road.

Here's the thing about running away from patterns: They're never going to magically stop unless you stop the cycle, stop the madness. It's up to you to get proactive and create a positive shift. I tell my clients all the time, "You are the singular most important person in your life and in your business. You need to prioritize accordingly." Who you want to be and what you want to create isn't going to magically happen through osmosis. It's a process, it's a step-by-step journey.

Part of my role in working with my clients is to give them permission to have that space to reevaluate and shift self-defeating behaviors. When they do that, instead of throwing up their hands and feeling trapped with no way out, as soon as they get that they're the one in control, it removes so much unneeded stress from their lives. Then it's just a matter of revisiting the system of, "This is what you want. These are the resources that you have. So now, let's start creating a process around that and then fill in the blanks as we go along."

If your underlying belief is, "What if I am not enough?" then you must be willing to undergo another process that will help you understand that you're the only person who's going to take you where you want to go. Sure, you can have all of the coaches, mentors, investments, and resources you can afford, but you have to realize that it all boils down to this: the common denominator is YOU.

Who is going to help me get what I want?

At the end of this chapter I will give you some action steps so you can identify what you want from your business, but first some tough love—no matter what you decide is your true north, you can't do it alone. As women, we almost always feel compelled to do it completely on our own, or that we should have the knowledge to do everything necessary. The minute we figure out that we don't, we completely stop ourselves.

P.S. I'm talking about my past self here. I always tried to suck it up and go full steam ahead thinking, "No, I got this. It's cool, I'll get it." Facepalm.

Building a support team isn't just smart, it's the only way to truly get what you want. You need to build a team of people who have expertise in the areas that you are "not so much" an expert in. But in order to create that team, you must know what you need from them, which is based on what you want along with a self-evaluation of your strengths.

This team is going to strengthen what I call your "not so much" areas which then allows you to focus on developing your zone of genius, all of which are all aligned with the end goal of achieving what you want. Don't worry we will prioritize what those are in later chapters so you will know exactly what those strengths are and what that first support is.

Who do I want to work with?

When you know who you **don't** want to work with, this will give you a sharper focus on who you **do** want to work with. Who gets you excited and motivates you? Who do you want to spend your time and energy on that will give you that profitability (mentally, emotionally, and financially) back?

This is your business, after all. You didn't start it to get stuck inside some metaphorical revolving door that you hate every minute of every single day. It's only natural that some days are going to suck—and I'm not going to glaze over that, either. But having those ideal clients all day, every day gives you the excitement and motivation to do the other things that don't bring you the same amount of instant profitability.

Once you get that clarity, it will be reflected in everything you do, including networking. You'll find that it actually just becomes ridiculously easy because now you have perfect focus on what you want, where you want to go, and who you want to talk to. Now you're armed with a dynamic conversation starter, not just the old implied, "Hi, I'm in the room, and I'm just here taking up space."

I hope you find benefit from my Bonus Page. I want to stress that if for any reason my methods don't click for you, don't let that stop you. If you don't receive the help you're seeking from me, then I encourage you to seek it out from other sources. Perhaps you're not in a position to afford to hire a coach right now. If that's the case, why not create a mutual accountability partnership with a friend so that you help each other stay focused on your specific goals. (i.e., keep reminding your partner to ask, "What do I really want?")

RECAP

- You have everything inside of you to answer the call of your soul, you just have to find it.

- To find it, you need to define what YOU want.

- Don't be afraid of things changing, because they will, but it will create a stronger, more successful YOU!

- These will help you create a profitable team to help you get what you want ON TOP OF your ideal client.

ACTION STEPS

- **Get what YOU want, out of your head.**

  - Brain dump on a piece of paper, journal, Google Doc, WHATEVER.

- **Narrow that down to what you want to accomplish in the next six months.**

  - Post it somewhere where you will see it every day. This is your true north and will help you reverse-engineer every month/every day.

CHAPTER 3

STEP #2:
TAME YOUR TIME

WHAT WE WILL BE covering in this chapter:

- How you can:
  - Control the time that you have.
  - Create boundaries around that time.
  - Identify how you are stealing from yourself in Time and Money.

You have FULL SAY on how you spend the time that you have.

Read. That. Again.

I understand that we all have responsibilities that we need to take care of. However, there is always time left and you have full say on how you spend that time. In the last chapter we identified what you wanted, now let's create the time to achieve it!

MY STORY

As I mentioned before, I am mom to an amazing boy named Max, who is on the Autism spectrum. Being his mom has taught me more about "time management" than any other mentor in my entire life. Because Autism is on a spectrum, not all autistic people share the same qualities and characteristics. For my son, his big ones are struggles with transitions from one activity to another, so routines and timers are his lifeline, and to be honest, are now mine as well.

Here is another truth, I thought I was a pretty patient person, but MAN, being his mom, broke that down and built it back even stronger! Not only patience with him, but also with myself. This has become critical in my growth as a business owner/entrepreneur.

My go-to time management/organization tactic used to be completely reactionary. I would jump from one thing to another, procrastinate like a mofo and get by, by the skin of my teeth. I used to tell myself, "Don't worry, there is a method to my madness." And you know what? It worked, for the most part. I got pretty much everything done and I stayed afloat.

Afloat. Not ahead.

Now enter Max. This phenomenal kiddo does not do well with "organized chaos." He needs to know what's on the agenda, when it's going to happen, a fair warning of when things are going to change, and he needs you to walk him through it at least three to four times, both before we start and throughout the day. So, my "go-to" planning needed to shift.

As moms, it is so easy to lose ourselves in this role: to completely adjust everything around our children, and slowly but surely lose the connection to what we want and the control over the time that we have. For some we consciously make that decision when our children are born, and I am not knocking that at all. But for me, and others, it was a progression that silently and slowly killed me.

The first year of being a mom was the hardest year of my life. I had dreamed of being a mom since I was a little girl and built up this idea in my head of how beautiful and easy it was going to be. Yeah… not so much. I was lost. I was tired. I was alone. I didn't have any family in Chicago. My husband was working crazy hours at the time and I was the only one in my group of friends who had a child.

Slowly but surely, I worked my way out of it, but it was another blow when my son was recognized as being on the autism spectrum at age three and a half. For those who haven't experienced something like this, there is a process of grief and acceptance that follows. But I learned more about myself as that process continued and still continues to this day. But a mother's guilt is real. With that guilt came small changes in my priorities until I realized I was putting his needs/wants first all the time. Then another small step created an additional OHF moment.

My son is an early riser, always has been, probably always will be. I am also a morning person. When I recognized that, I wanted to create more time in my day (Hello, Step #1!). I decided to set a morning alarm with the intention of waking up at least one hour before Max. That first morning I woke up with my alarm, excited to have this extra quiet time to myself and guess who also woke up? Yup, it was Max. (Fuuuuuuck) So what did I do?

I got mad, got him out of his room, and completely negated what I had planned in order to sit with him while he ate breakfast and did his morning play time. Another fun Max fact: once he gets into a mode, he is engrossed in it and could really give two shits if I am in the same room as him as long as he knows where I am so he can find me when needed.

For WEEKS said fact was apparent to me and yet I CHOSE to still sit with him and be mad that I didn't get to do what I wanted to do. Facepalm again.

Then one day the OHF hit me and I realized that he didn't have a say over my time, I did. He wasn't asking for my time; I purely just gave it up because I thought that was the right thing to do. But I have a choice and full say.

The next time he woke up before or with my alarm, I got him situated with his breakfast and morning activity. Then I told him I was going to be in my room for the next thirty minutes. He briefly looked up from his breakfast and said, "Okay, Momma," and I went ahead with my morning plan.

To this day he still knows this routine: if he wakes up before I am done with my morning plans, I go in to say good morning, give him a kiss, help him with breakfast and then let him know when I will be done with my work.

It's the little things you do every day that make the biggest difference.

"You have FULL SAY on how you spend the time that you have."

Graduate From Multitasking Into Being A Maestro

Are you a major multitasker? If so, good for you, but I want to point something out here. There is a difference between multitasking and working on things in parallel. When you're operating in parallel, you still have your energy focused on the here and now. Then, when you're done with that path, you proceed to your next focus, which is a parallel move.

Reinventing your approach this way means you're not doing five things at once and sinking into overwhelm. Because anytime you try to tackle that many projects simultaneously, you'll soon find that you're doing everything half-assed.

That fosters sporadic, disconnected thinking. Distractions create that, too. A little tip that I share with clients is so simple but so powerful. While you're focused on a project, just turn off all of your notifications on your phone during that time. Just by doing that, you'll stay sharper and become more productive.

Because when we have that phone in our line of sight while we're writing or designing something, the truth of the matter is you're not multitasking more. Rather, you're distracting yourself. You're procrastinating is what you're doing. It's a term that I call "subconscious procrastination."

Those are the kinds of things we don't necessarily categorize as procrastination. We see it as being, "Well, I was productive today." My checkpoint response to that is, "Okay, but were you profitable? Where are you financially?"

You must give yourself permission to become a Maestro. Think about the maestro who conducts an orchestra. She/he leads multiple sections of instrumentalists, and by working in complete harmony, focused on the maestro's direction, something moving and beautiful results from their combined efforts. So, I encourage you to step up to the podium, if you will, raise your baton (your expertise), and lead your musicians (resource/support people) in manifesting something amazing.

Some of my clients have called me a "Superwoman" and when I hear that, I actually cringe. They mean well, it's an attempt at a compliment when they say, "Oh, yeah, you should work with Mel. She's a Superwoman!" But if I hear that, I immediately respond by objecting, "No, I'm not!"

Even if you look at all of the women who have attained massive success, like Oprah, you need to bear in mind that she took her success as far as she could on her own, and then she wisely reached out to enlist that first resource to help enhance her "not so much" area.

I love telling my clients who have a tendency to compare themselves to famous "Superwomen"—"Hey! Here's the deal. You have the same twenty-four hours as Beyoncé, but Beyoncé has an assistant, a shopper, a personal trainer, and the list goes on and on. Of course, you aren't operating at the same level as Beyoncé! You don't have the team she does, so give yourself a break!" Then we begin talking about building their team using whatever resources they have at the moment.

*TERA'S STORY

Tera is a sex and intimacy coach who helps women struggle with overthinking and undervaluing themselves in their relationships. I met this amazing woman during one of my workshops in Chicago. This workshop was a breakdown of this book and gave them time to really delve into their goals and create customized, prioritized plans of action. Her OHF moment came when I walked them through an exercise that showed them how they were stealing time and money from themselves by procrastinating. (Don't worry! I'll walk you through it as well in a minute.)

A week later, I ran into her at another networking event. As soon as she saw me, she got the biggest smile, grabbed my arm, and had me sit down with her while squealing, "I've got to show you something!"

After we sat down, she went into her bag and pulled out her planner. "Look!" she exclaimed. As I looked at her planner, I saw her whole month mapped out, not only with her monthly goals but also broken down into weekly and daily actions. I have to admit it was so fucking pretty!

"Every morning, I wake up and look at this and just feel so relieved! It's all there! And if something comes up that isn't aligned with my focus that day, I can see if/when I can fit it in and confidently say yes or no."

The look of pride and confidence on Tera's face made my entire week! THAT'S why I do this. It is so amazing when talented women like Tera treat themselves and their time with the confidence and tenacity they deserve.

A few more weeks later, she emailed me to celebrate the fact that things that have been on her to-do list for months—and some for years—have been handled while she continued to build her business AND author a book.

"This was so simple to implement."

See, simple.

Things on her to do list for months/years have been handled, or they are in progress while she runs her business AND authors a book. Simple and easy for her to implement.

Time Taming Obstacles

We've established that you need to know, "What do I want?" That's your true north. Now, where is the time to get you there? When I pose this question to clients, no one has ever told me the actual answer. They typically go into great detail about all of these little things that are pulling them away from pursuing what they want. Often it boils down to procrastination, which is such an umbrella term.

Bottom line? Procrastination is nothing but fear. It's a fear of success, fear of failure, and most of the time it's fear of the unknown. That's really the core root of procrastination. It's not that you just don't want to stay on track. There's something deeper.

Sometimes you can connect to it and you still ignore it. Other times you tell yourself, "I don't know why, but I just don't want to do that. So, I'm going to do something else." Lots of people say, "I'm such a perfectionist. I need to have XYZ perfect before I do that." But I call them out on that by telling them, "Now you're not being a perfectionist, you're just being a procrastinator."

It's become a vicious cycle.

First, let's take the emotion out of it. Instead of looking at your day like, "Oh, my God, I have all of this shit to do and no time," here's what I recommend:

Look at your schedule and figure out, "Okay, I have this much time. What do I want to fill it with?" That reframing instantly puts you on the path away from overwhelm and closer to success. It also gives you more clarity so you have the confidence to start saying no to those *good* things so that you can leave yourself open for the *best*.

It's those little mind-flips that rob us of our day all the time. I've been there myself, and I'm willing to bet that you often find yourself waking up and starting each day by asking yourself, "How am I supposed to get this all done today?"

Looking at your schedule as you plunge into your day, you're already stressed out and racking your brain wondering how you're going to get everything done before your day has even started! Why not stop that habit right now? I like to say, "Just nip it in the bud!" Allow a mind-flip to help you consider a more productive way to begin and live your day.

If you find yourself in the same boat of feeling overextended, I'd like to give you a challenge that actually is a pretty quick fix. I've found that the main reason women, in particular, find themselves there is because they tend to say yes to everything. That typically comes from one's upbringing, as well as having spent years of worrying about lack.

I'm talking about a lack of customers, lack of money, lack of opportunity, and ad infinitum. So, they say yes to everything. Then the perfect opportunity will come along and they can't take it because they're so overextended with all these little yeses.

If this applies to you, here's a quick check-in question I invite you to ask yourself: "Is what I'm doing helping me to be profitable? Mentally, emotionally, and/or financially toward what I want?" If the answer has even an inkling of, "No," then here's the next step:

Take a look at your calendar and figure out when you can schedule some of those activities that aren't advancing you towards your goal *after* you're done with the things you want to do to get to where you want. It's not like you have to completely cut yourself off from everybody, be a bitch, and say no to everything. It's a matter of prioritizing, but always remember, "I am first."

We All Can Get Stuck in Routines that are Counter-productive

You've done it, I've certainly done it. There are so many times we get stuck in routines. The story I shared above highlights that. We get caught up in a routine of even simple things. One day I was talking to one of my clients, we were looking at her calendar to create time for herself and her business and I asked, "Well, what about Thursday night? Can you do some work on Thursday night?" She answered, "No, that's date night with my husband."

So, I said, "Oh, great! What are you doing?" She said, "Oh, we actually just have the TV on and sit next to each other and we're both on our phones the whole time." I paused and considered that then said, "Okay. Is that something that is really a non-negotiable reason? Do you feel like this is something that is elevating your relationship or supporting your relationship?" She said, "No, we just do it because we've always done it."

I thought about that for a moment before I replied, "Okay. Well, if that is how you two have structured it, what could you do XYZ on your phone super-quick since you guys are both on your phone? Or do you make that a non-negotiable to where you don't have your phone? Maybe you guys turn your phones off and go for a walk. Make it kind of shorter, with more quality combined."

My point that I stressed to my client was, "Why not use your date night routine to make it more concise for what you want out of that time so you can spend the time you have left on your priorities?"

If date night with your partner is profitable to you both mentally and emotionally, then that is definitely the *best* you need to say yes to. But if not, how can you shift it so it can be? I'm not saying you need to neglect your relationships to be successful, but I definitely encourage you to evaluate how they are supporting you and the life you want to have.

Procrastination: The Thief of Time and Money

I mentioned in *Tera's story that I did an exercise that provided her a OHF moment that helped her tame the time that she had. Now, I'm not a mental health professional, but I have had years of practice analyzing my own procrastination as well as that of my clients. And I've deduced that there are two different types of procrastination: conscious and subconscious.

Conscious procrastination is when you internally and mentally beat yourself up for not doing something you know you should be doing as you're scrolling through Facebook, going through Instagram, or watching that seventh episode of Lord knows what on Netflix.

Even while you're involved in that distracting activity, you're telling yourself, "I shouldn't be doing this." But you keep scrolling, watching, etcetera, even though you know you shouldn't because by doing that activity, you are purposely neglecting doing something to help you grow in your business. That's conscious procrastination.

Subconscious procrastination is trickier for women, especially. Here the process of procrastination easily kicks in when we make ourselves overly available to others. By that, I mean being helpful and supportive to others to our own detriment. So, this is going way beyond self-value and amounts to trying to get validation that you're a good person from others, or whatever that side conversation is with yourself that you're trying to fill.

We rationalize helping others because we tend to see it as, "I don't have a choice because I need to help my friend," or "I can't do this today because now I have to…." Well, here's a shocker. You can still say, "No" or you can say, "Not right now." More on that in the exercise below. Hopefully you're wondering, "What's the solution, Mel?"

Let's start with the little things because, remember, doing those every day make the biggest difference: Turn off all your notifications on your phone.

No beeps.
No banners.
No nothing.

We're just like Pavlov's dogs with those suckers. As soon as we hear that, "Bing!" we leap to check it out. "Oh, somebody liked us on Instagram?" It just goes downhill from there because we don't necessarily see that as procrastination right off the bat.

Turn off all your notifications.

Really, do you want to create a do not disturb environment so you can hone in on something? Turn on "Do Not Disturb" on your phone. This means your mom can't call you, or your best friend can't text you with a funny little video. Of course, if it's a do-or-die situation, they can always get through. But again, it's those little things, those boundaries that are really going to help you tame your time because you're giving yourself permission to truly focus on what you need to do.

The next phase is a little trickier. This usually dovetails off of the silencing of notifications. Women often ask me, "How do I deal with the guilt of taking time for myself?" The thing is, it's not going to instantly go away. You're not going to feel magically empowered because you said no to your mom or your best friend. You're going to feel guilty. However, what you're doing is you're reestablishing your boundaries. Now, this can get interesting because, initially, you might get pushback from some friends. I did.

When I started laser-focusing on myself and my business, it caused major changes in relationships, including my marriage. But those were changes for the better and I'm grateful I made them.

So, nope. It's not instantaneous, but the more you start seeing what you can create for yourself, and the more that your friends and your family members also witness that, then it becomes a new level of empowerment. It's this whole new elation, a whole new superpower that you have.

That's when the guilt starts getting less and less and less. Because again, you're not saying, "No, I'm unavailable blah, blah, blah..." You're just saying, "Not right now. I can't help you right now, but I can call you back in fifteen minutes when I'm done with this." Or "I can't help you move today, but I can come over in two days and help you unpack."

You can still be of value and of service to others, just not to the detriment of yourself. That is bullshit. Here's a funny way to look at this, because humor always softens change. Think of this as if you are going from being a mistress to the time to being the master of the time. Pretty cool, huh?

When I was married, I always used to joke around that his job was the wife and I was the mistress. What I meant was, I always felt like I wasn't really my husband's top priority. So, another "OHF" landed when I asked myself, "Who can make me a priority?" *I* can. Once I realized that, it was a matter of figuring out what I could start doing to make myself a priority and create as much as I can for myself instead of having to completely rely on others to fulfill that for me.

My friend and publisher Melissa pointed out that there are these huge things that people can fall into, and it's almost like falling into a ditch. There's the ditch of guilt, the ditch of then having problems with feeling selfish, and so on. When she pointed that out, it reminded me of a quote that basically goes, "The difference between a ditch and a grave is that a ditch is open-ended. You're not closed off when you're in a ditch. You can always get out and keep moving. But in a grave, you're stuck."

I know it sounds horrible on some levels, but we women tend to be really great at digging our own graves. If you find that this is something you do, I encourage you to do one simple thing: "Stand up!" (Either metaphorically or combined with doing it physically. That can really get your blood and creativity flowing on all levels!)

Just stand up! Then you can see over the edge and survey your options as you climb out of that ditch. But if you just keep laying down and keep digging, then that creates heavy negative tunnel vision. Doing nothing really *is* moving backward. Either you're going to step forward, or crawl out of that and start building, versus digging yourself into holes.

As I mentioned earlier in this book, my first business was working as a personal trainer in the fitness industry. When my clients would complain that they didn't have enough time to devote to their exercise regimen, I used to tell them all the time:

"Something is better than nothing and nothing is not an option."

And that applies to getting a grip on how you spend your time in whatever area you may be struggling.

Women tend to grapple with recognizing the difference between being selfish and practicing self-care. It's a nuance, but it's not as subtle as you might think at first. Because when most people put themselves in the category of being selfish, that becomes a bad thing. "Oh, this is all my fault. I'm so selfish."

The word "selfish" is such an interesting term to me, because bottom line is that to get ahead in this world you need to be selfish. At least on a certain level. Why? Because nobody else is going to give you what you want. You have to know what you want so you can ask for it. Some people might even define *that* act as being selfish; saying and/or writing down, "This is what I want, this is what I need, these are my expectations." But I'm here to tell you, that is NOT selfish. It's just creating what you want, being proactive in your life.

When I think of somebody who is selfish, I tend to look at that as somebody who is deliberately choosing not to give two shits about anybody else. Doesn't matter who they beat up, doesn't matter who they walk over, it doesn't matter what they talk about. They just don't care. They just want to get what they want. That's selfish. To me, identifying what you want, asking for what you want, and creating a life that you want is simply being proactive. That's simply a factor of being present.

This bears repeating: Nobody else is going to do it for you. Besides, why would you want to tell somebody even in the vaguest of terms what you want, and then just hand it completely over to them and just sit back? If you did that, it's never going to be what *you* truly want. It's never going to be perfect. Even what you want now is going to be completely different down the road, but when you allow yourself to take the time to have that say, you're immersed in that journey. You're changing it, you're building on it.

You're not just letting shit ride and then either bitching and moaning that it didn't get done the way you wanted it to, or complaining that it's not happening fast enough. That's where blaming it on other people comes into play and you put yourself in the role of a martyr or victim. But the truth is, the responsibility of taking control falls right on your own shoulders.

When you first begin your journey toward personally accomplishing your goals, in the beginning, you have a vision of how that could wind up looking. That vision may be a bit murky from the initial steps you take, but the journey gets clearer and clearer as your vision grows. When you're at this stage and setting up boundaries, the concept of self-care enters the picture, too. A great example of this is in Maslow's hierarchy of needs, which is a theory that shows how we partake in behavioral motivation. Maslow used the terms "physiological", "safety", "belonging and love", "social needs" or "esteem", and "self-actualization" to describe the pattern through which human motivations generally move. This means that in order for motivation to arise at the next stage, each stage must be satisfied within the individual themselves.

CliffsNotes version: in order to have the motivation to help others, you gotta tick off your boxes first!

People can easily lock themselves into non-growth and non-action because they allow themselves to be paralyzed by fear. When that happens, they're not going to grow, develop, or create new things that they can give as gifts.

Here's a quick analogy: A genuinely selfish person would grow a garden and eat everything herself, but then she'd wind up with nobody to perhaps help her create a better garden and nobody to share anything with. People wouldn't want to have exchanges with her in that case. If you don't really grow yourself, you're actually limiting yourself from realizing all the gifts that you could give, and also the additional and better gifts you could both give and receive.

With regard to prioritizing your time, that includes self-care. Going back to the "Aha!" exercise of turning off your notifications, it will help you to understand and laser in on making your time as productive as possible. This helps you take a non-emotional look at where your time is being spent. So, you have then identified what subconscious procrastination is versus conscious procrastination. And let's face it, when someone uses that old saying that "Time is money," this is exactly what they mean.

OHF! Procrastination Exercise

Now that you know the difference between subconscious and conscious procrastination grab a pen and paper, because you need to see this in black and white, not just in your mind's eye. Studies have shown that when you write an idea down on pen and paper it actually becomes more tangible for us[2] and that people who write and/or visualize their dreams and goals vividly range between 1.2 and 1.4 times more likely to achieve those goals and dreams than those who do not write them down.

Look at your last full week of work and write down how many hours you consciously and subconsciously procrastinated during that week.

Got it?

That's how much time you stole from yourself that week.

But "time is money," right?

Now multiply that number by how much you charge an hour.

---

2   Murphy, Mark. "Neuroscience Explains Why You Need to Write Down Your Goals if You Actually Want to Achieve Them." Forbes. April 15, 2018. https://www.forbes.com/sites/markmurphy/2018/04/15/neuroscience-explains-why-you-need-to-write-down-your-goals-if-you-actually-want-to-achieve-them/#65db3ba47905

That's how much time and money you've stolen from yourself during that week. Next, multiply that by four: that's every month. Now times that by twelve. That's every year.

Believe me, I'm not saying you're going to magically get all of that time and money back, but what if you can get at least a quarter of it back? What would you be able to accomplish with that extra time and money? What adventures would you be able to go on, what would you be able to develop in your business? What would you be able to do if you had a quarter of that back or half of that back? Even three-quarters of it back?

Your final figure may throw you for a loop, but that's okay. Realize that none of us is perfect. I still procrastinate. But I do it a lot less than I did seven years ago, and my business now reflects that. In fact, my business and my life.

It's the little things you do, every day, that make the biggest difference, and you have full say on how you spend the time that you have.

RECAP

- You have full say on how you spend the time you have.

- Don't do things out of routine; evaluate who and what takes your time as well as how you are benefiting from it.

- There are two types of procrastination—subconscious and conscious. Both are stealing time and money from you.

ACTION STEPS

- Create boundaries for your time by:

  - Turning off notifications

  - Utilizing DO NOT DISTURB when you want to hone in on a task

  - Create office hours. You don't have twenty-four hours a day to work your business so stop acting like it.

- Download the "Tame Your Time" bonus located at the end of this book!

CHAPTER 4

STEP #3:
PRIORITIZE YOUR TASKS

WHAT WE WILL COVER in this chapter:

- Understanding:
  - The importance of knowing what is on your to-do list and why it's on there.
  - Simple tips to ensure you are prioritizing your time correctly.
  - It's possible to feel successful every day, no matter how much time you have.

Before you go any further you need to make sure you have identified what you want (i.e. your true north) and the time that you have. Because I am now going to show you how to create a prioritized plan of action that will work inside of the time you have. In this way every day, no matter how much time you have, you are always taking steps toward creating the business, money, and life you want!

MY STORY

Few things in this world make me feel happier or more "productive" than a to-do list. I tell my friends/family/clients all the time, "If it's not on the list, it won't get done." But, like most of us, in the beginning my "to-do" list was a never-ending list of every single thing I ever thought of that I need to do for myself, my son, my clients, etc. Before I started developing and utilizing this system, that list became my friend and my foe.

The first mistake I would always make is to try to complete them in order. And by "in order" I mean the easy stuff first, for everyone else, and my stuff at the bottom. Because that would help me feel productive. Guess what? Productive does not equal PROFITABLE—mentally, emotionally, or financially. This was a major contributor to being so busy but being so poor, as I mentioned in my story in Chapter 1.

Another mistake I would make is I wouldn't break up large tasks into bite-sized pieces. I kept backing myself into a corner by convincing myself that certain tasks would take "all day" and I was just waiting for that day to come.

Sound familiar?

Shockingly, that day NEVER came! I know, right?!

So every day, for the first seven years of being an entre-preneur, this was my life: wake up, look at my MASSIVE to-do list, stress out, have coffee, do the little things/easy things so I can say I did something (and NONE of those were for me or my business), then look back at my list, see the large things that are still on there, tell myself I don't have enough time, and then procrastinate. All the while feeling guilty that I should do more, and expecting better results.

One of my favorite fitness trainers, Autumn Calabrese, always says, "You can't be mad at the results you didn't get by the work you didn't do."

I shared that first real moment I took control of my business in Chapter 1. Now I am going to share how I have evolved that into what I do now, every day.

TURNING THE DREADED "TO-DO" LIST INTO AN ADVANTAGE

I am going to safely assume that, like my past self, you have an ongoing To-Do List. I am also going to safely assume that more than half of that list is probably not even remotely connected to what you actually want right now in your business. Yes, you can have a "master" to-do list where you can brain-dump everything you THINK you need to do to be successful. I already showed how much that increases your odds of success.

Now let's prioritize this sucker.

"You have to schedule your priorities, not prioritize your schedule."

So just to review, (this is going to start to feel like a well-loved song pretty soon!) First, you have to know what you want. Then, recognize the time you have, and then from there, which one(s) of your tasks sit within that timeline?

For those of you who have more than ten things on your To-Do List, I'm already telling you that's not going to cut it.

Cut it down.

Way down.

Shoot for just three. Yes, three. If you can confidently say you have more time in a given day you can make it five, TOPS. These are your "Do-or-Die" items. As in your business will DIE if you do not get them done today. A bit dramatic? Nope, because the more days you continue to not get shit done, the closer you are to killing your business and taking your mental, emotional, and financial health with it.

DO NOT let your To-Do list become a procrastination device. We have already established what that takes from you in the last chapter.

Here is an example of a To-Do list you have created:
1. Contact five clients.
2. Shoot out ten emails.
3. Fill out a contract.
4. Walk the dog.
5. Do the dishes.
6. Go grocery shopping.

Be honest, which ones do you do first?

Walk the dog, do the dishes, and go grocery shopping, right?

I understand and validate that crossing things off your list gives you a rush like no other. In fact, the neurotransmitters of dopamine and serotonin get involved in our physicality. These two regulate similar bodily functions, but the effects they create are quite different. Dopamine regulates mood and muscle activity, as well as plays a major role in the brain's pleasure and reward systems. Serotonin helps regulate mood, body temperature, appetite, and sleep patterns. I have clients that actually put stuff on their list that they already did JUST so they can cross it off! I'm not knocking that because it's real, however, how much more excited and energized would you feel if those "Do-or-Die" items were done first?

Yes, you are being productive but are you being profitable mentally, emotionally, or financially? Is that actually helping you make money? The last time I checked, dogs don't pay the bills.

Come on. You *know* you have to walk the dog; they are going to remind you. You *know* that you have to go grocery shopping because you are going to get hungry and you *know* you need to do the dishes because they are going to start smelling. You have outside reminders to help you get this shit done therefore, you really don't need those on your list.

When it comes to your business items, most of us aren't privy to having those outside reminders. This has to come from you.

Moral of the story:

Take your personal shit off of your business to-do list.

OTHERS' STORIES

I love working with creatives. I know how their brain works, because mine is very similar. They get inspired by so many ideas and, without much thought, they instantly start working on them, whether it makes sense or not.

They are driven by passion and the excitement of that "next thing." They don't do monotony.

Abby was no exception. Abby is a painter as well as a founder of a tutoring company. When we first met, she had multiple ideas that she was trying to implement all at once: a blog series, a podcast, a course, being consistent in her social media, and building her emailing list. She was overwhelmed and tired of never completing a task that actually gave her an ROI—mentally, emotionally, or financially.

So, what we did first is establish what she wanted to create with her business: her primary focus was to get X amount of 1:1 clients to get her to a monthly financial base.

Then we looked at how much time she wanted to spend with clients as well as on her business. (Remember you have FULL SAY on how you spend your time and there are no rules to how much that needs to be, per day, to be successful. I have full proof of that!)

With that goal in mind, we looked at all of her tasks and prioritized them so we could see how some of them actually rolled into one another. By creating a content calendar, she was able to spend more time on her blogs, which gave her more content to share on social media.

Another client of mine said that we needed to talk about the three avenues that she had to prioritize to create her biggest profit results. Those three avenues were:

- Her time
- Her effort
- Herself

She asked me, "Which of those three do you think is my biggest profit avenue?" And of course, the answer is always YOU! This is your business, and you are the singular most important person in your business. That's why I say I help women prioritize themselves *correctly*, from their personal core. My first business back in 2010 was in the fitness industry and, physically, you need a strong core or else your body is not going to work at its fullest capacity.

Take great care of yourself on all levels because without health, there is no wealth.

The same goes for yourself and your business. If you don't continually take the time to strengthen yourself, you will never create the business, money, and life that you want.

I have found many fitness parallels when it comes to building a business. Here is another one: just like in fitness, you can't spot train and expect the full results. Your business is stabilized by many muscles, or funnels. You have to train everything to work in tandem to get the results that you want. It's the same principle of prioritizing your tasks on every level.

For example, if exercise is going to be a priority in your life, then that needs to be another non-negotiable, which goes back to Tame Your Time. In that case, you need to schedule that into your day, every day. Since that is already a scheduled priority, you don't need to put that on your To-Do List.

To illustrate this a bit further, I chatted with someone during a networking event who said, "My main focus is my health first and then my business." So I told her, "Okay, so in your weekly schedule, block out the dates/times you want to work out, then you build your schedule around that."

BREAK, BREAK IT DOWN!

I want to remind you how vital it is to focus on prioritizing your tasks. It's all about honing in on what are the "Do-or-Dies" that you need to accomplish. As I said earlier, those should be limited to no more than three things a day. Because the other tasks are things you already know what to do or how to do it, like answering emails. These don't need to be on your To-Do List because they should already be in your schedule. They are a part of your regular daily routine.

When you walk into your space, your office, or what have you, it always goes back to identifying what you want. You now know the time you have every day, and now you just need to make sure that everything that's in front of you helps you get to what you want. To make your To-Do List one of your most valuable resources, you need to prioritize nothing but what you want. Period. That way you don't get distracted, you don't procrastinate on something that doesn't matter because it's not in front of your face.

Out of sight, out of mind.

You can start with the To-Do list that you currently have, and just move the right ones to the top. You could do this for a whole month, if you like, in order to reach your monthly goal of X.

A common question I get is, "Which is better to stay prioritized, pen and paper list or electronic list?"

To which I ALWAYS answer, "Whichever one works best for you!" You know how you work best, and I never, ever try to change that; I help you change what is NOT working.

"If it ain't broke, don't fix it."

I use an electronic app called Any.do. It's crazy simple, just how I like it. It is broken up into four categories: Today, Tomorrow, Upcoming, and Someday.

Someday is my Master List.

When I recognize what I want to accomplish for the month I move those correlating tasks into my Upcoming List.

Then I distribute those throughout the week into my Today and Tomorrow list.

Every month or so, I'll review my Someday list and think, "Why is this even on here? This isn't even applicable!" or I'll ask myself, "Did I really forget about this? And do I want to move it because things have shifted from when I first thought of it six months ago?" Now it's actually next month, so I need to move that up to the top of my Someday list and then that's the first thing for next month.

You may discover that you need to break down some of the tasks because, otherwise, it will become too overwhelming. If that's the case, go ahead and break them down into smaller steps.

Let's say that your goal for June is, "I want to launch my website." You want to accomplish all of your To-Dos that you feel you have to, need to, want to do to produce a successful website by the end of June. Then you would. Need to prioritize those out, even the detailed stuff like, "I need to decide what I want my website to be about." Okay, great. What do you need to decide about that?

Then break those down so that you really can see everything that's involved. For some people, that starts to sound and feel extremely overwhelming. They thought they had four things, but now they see they really have fifteen things.

The focus to maintain throughout this is that you're taming the time that you have. So instead of procrastinating because you don't have enough time to get everything you want done, wouldn't you feel more profitable if, by the end of the day, you've been focused on choosing your theme or center for your website? And you knew at the beginning of the day that you needed to finish up those first five things. So, you just knocked them out.

You see, you're not actually creating more tasks; what you're doing is creating a step-by-step process where you focus on that next step to get over onto your big picture. It's just the first step. That one's done, now what's the next step? Oh, look! Now I have my entire theme for my website. Now what's the next big thing I want to get done, and how do I break that down within the time that I have?

I think one of the problems that women especially have, is that we just want to get it done. My mom is like that with cleaning. Her famous words are, "I just want to get it done. I'll feel better," or, "I'll sleep better if I know I just got it done." But I also know cleaning isn't her favorite (let me tell you right now, the apple doesn't fall far from the tree), so I would hear her talking to herself when I was home that she needs to get this done but then would find herself doing something else. I know now that if she hadn't gotten so wound up about it, the cleaning she was doing would probably only have taken thirty minutes, tops. But it dragged out because she was emotionally overwhelmed.

You can have that attitude if you really want to, but instead of getting all worked up about it and putting pressure on yourself, thinking, "I have to get everything done right NOW!" couldn't it be better if you had just three little things on your list?

I believe that by using a productivity strategy that lets you whittle those items that have to do with your business and profitability into doable pieces every day, you also build something akin to a muscle of accomplishment. You're building a habit and then creating a natural reward when you hit your goal. When you do that, you're not working yourself to a bone for three weeks and then feeling completely exhausted, only to start that old routine all over again.

What I'm teaching you to do is actually a lifestyle.

All my clients tend to feel uncomfortable at first when they go through the process of breaking tasks down. It might sound more exhausting than it really is on the surface, but just like any other muscle, when you start to work it, it exhausts you really quickly. You just have to build that endurance as you go along in creating smaller bits and pieces for your tasks.

Delegation & Automation: Your New BFFS

Delegating is definitely a key element when it comes to prioritizing. Whether you're a solo-preneur or a leader, you need to know what your strengths are, and what your "not so much" areas are.

Delegation is huge.

From my years of experience working with female clientele, I've learned that it's a common theme that women suck at it! I sucked at it! But I've gotten better. One part of it is the belief that we need to prove we did this on our own. That we can do it all and then some. Another part is the fact that some of us (Hi, that's me!) get skittish about giving the control to someone else.

To help me ease into this area I actually started with delegating things OUTSIDE of my business so I could create more time for it.

Those two things were a cleaning lady (told you I hated cleaning) and grocery delivery. Eliminating those two tasks added an average of six hours to my week. Is the grocery delivery a bit more expensive than going to the store?

Yup, but let's actually look at the "cost." I live in the city of Chicago and therefore don't have a car and my closest grocery store is a half-mile away. Now, I have to be very cognitive of what I buy because momma has to carry it home! So, I would actually go grocery-shopping multiple times a week. I also have a kiddo who HATES going to the grocery store because it over-stimulates him, so that means I need to take time out of my office time, while he is at school, to get this done. Therefore, I was losing about two hours a week.

Remember that exercise we did for procrastination?

That applies here as well. I figured I was out almost $500 per week by not being able to work, so, yeah, spending a little bit more on groceries makes sense in my situation.

Same with the cleaning lady. Why would I punish myself and be out of money when I can invest in another woman's business, who fucking loves it, does it better than I do AND in less time??

It's not about how much you are spending, it's what you are getting back in time and money, that matters.

Take inventory of what the things are in your personal life that you can delegate in order to give you more time for your business. It's a priority.

Now, in your business, is your "not so much" area something that you can work on in parallel to your strength? If that's the case, then identify what is the first step to strengthening that in the time that you have. Or, is it really just not in your wheelhouse? Then identify who or what you need to reach out to for help and support; or establish to just take it off your plate.

"You have the same twenty-four hours as Beyoncé."

Hashtag FACT truth, however: Beyoncé has multiple assistants, multiple nannies, multiple managers, and so on and so forth. Tame your time and delegate!

AUTOMATION
Automation is one of those "little things" that make a big difference and is designed to make your life simpler. So, use it whenever you can!

The first one that creates more time is creating a scheduling link for your calls. There are many to choose from: Calendly, Acuity, etc. This elevates so much time and energy you probably didn't know you were using playing a seemingly endless game of phone and/or email tag just to schedule an appointment.

Tame your time even more by creating your scheduling link to schedule calls only on certain days at certain times. This lets people know when you're available and they can sign up online to book their appointment with you. This decreases your back-and-forth communication as well as helps avoid double-booking.

If you're working strictly on your memory, odds are at some point you won't remember what time you said to what person. You're human, give yourself a break and automate!

For me, if I know that Tuesdays and Thursdays are the days I want to leave open for other phone calls, now I can look at my schedule and know that Mondays, Wednesdays, and Fridays I have full say on how you want to spend them, because they've been *boundaried* out.

Tame your time by only taking a certain number of calls during given times. I know some of you just tightly inhaled with the fear that you will miss out on something if you don't leave yourself open. That is not going to happen.

If an extremely important opportunity is really wanting to schedule time with you and doesn't see any availability in your calendar, they will contact you directly and you have full say on if/when you can put them in.

All of this helps you control your time and gives you that peace of mind so that you don't have to keep worrying about,

"Did I get back to that email? Did I say the right time?" or "I've got seven phone calls in one day. How did that happen?!?"

Honestly, tools like this help in giving yourself that permission to tame your time without the guilt factor.

What are the first things you can automate to alleviate some of that pressure and overwhelm?

I've seen it time and again with my clients who work my methodology. I know that if you apply it in your life, you will gain the experience of managing and securing boundaries for yourself so that you can have the kind of life where you don't feel guilty all the time.

You'll find that you have a successful, fulfilled life from Day 1.

No burnout required.

When you follow the process every day, even on the shit days, you know you took a step forward in your business because you made it a priority. Give yourself the permission to celebrate what you did achieve instead of beating yourself up for what you didn't.

You should never feel like you have to force shit to happen and wear yourself out in the process. I'm so tired of people who say, "Just push through it." My reply to that? Fuck you!

If I emotionally, physically, and mentally cannot produce anything, why, why, why would I want to force that? This is something it took me a long time to learn because I used to be horrible about that. But since shifting that mindset about eighteen months ago from the writing of this book, my business, my life, and myself have taken an incredibly positive 360-degree turn. When I feel done, I am done!

For example, is there something that I promised somebody I would do, and I know that it would affect their business if I didn't do it today? If the reality is that it's something I can do without a meeting or if it's just an email, then I stay in my pajamas, stay in my bed, have my comfy tea and I knock out that particular Do-or-Die task by the time I'm supposed to.

Going back to the first chapter, you need to know what you want in order to ask for that. Or to utilize that resource profitably. Trust me, you don't have to do five million things a day to be successful. It can even just be, "Hey! I answered my email today." Score! Or maybe you decided that this day is total shit. Nothing is working. Push everything to the next day. Even doing that gives you clarity on how much are you actually working.

Then you can do a little self-questionnaire and figure out, "What attributed to that?" Was it because you didn't set your boundaries? That, even though you have established you're only going to handle three calls a day, but you broke your own rules and took four? It's that same old answer: This is a process that always boils down to, "What do you want, what is the time you have, and what's going to fit in the time you have to get to what you want?"

RECAP

- Prioritize the tasks that are aligned with what you want.

- Prioritize three tasks each day.

- Take your personal shit off of your business to-do list.

- Work with your strengths.

- Delegation doesn't have to be something in your business.

- Recognize, reapply, and MOVE ON!

ACTION STEPS

- Create a prioritized list aligned with what you want to accomplish in the next thirty days.

- Schedule your Non-Negotiables and get them off your list.

- Implement a scheduling link to create more time to devote to your prioritized tasks.

CHAPTER 5

STEP #4:
CUSTOMIZE YOUR CALENDAR

WHAT WE WILL COVER in this chapter:

- How to:
    - Customize your plan for how you work and the time you have.
    - Still be successful when shit goes south.
    - Ensure you are working in alignment with what you want.

Some days are just never going to go as planned, and that's OK! This process is designed to ebb and flow with you so no matter how much time you have at a given day, you have a plan of action to crush it. I like to think of it as a variation of the game of Tetris. "This is what I want to accomplish today; this is how much time I have; I'm going to fit these actions into this timeframe."

MY STORY

As a parent, I know for a fact that a day can shoot to shit in a heartbeat. But the beautiful thing about this process is that even when things do shoot to shit, if you are energetically OK (and it's OK if you're not), you always have some time to devote to your business. It's just a matter of recognizing the time you have now, rearranging your priorities to fit into that time, applying that new plan of action, and moving on!

What's not OK is using that as an excuse to just think your entire day is screwed. Your entire day is not screwed if one thing changes it up. Remember, you still have full say on the time you have left. Now it's just rearranging your priorities to the time that you have so you can do what you want. This is creating a constant circular movement that you can always come back to and customize.

My son, Max, is a master traveler. I love traveling with this kid. His first flight, he was six weeks old and since then flies an average of four times per year with me or his dad. Even though this has become routine for him, it does not mean it saves us from meltdowns or over-stimulation, especially when we are visiting family and have a lot on the agenda. There have been multiple moments when I have had to put the customization step in full effect but this one time, when we were in Colorado, it was a kicker.

Max was seven at the time and we had flown into Denver for my Grandmother's funeral. Now my mom's side of the family is pretty big. My mom is one of four children, there are sixteen grandkids and, at the time, twenty-three great-grand-children. Yeah. My mom's family and my dad's family are ridiculously close as well, so that meant a lot of outings/events planned with a lot of people so we could all catch up and reconnect during this time. I also had some work calls that I wanted to take while I was there. Basically, the ingredients for a perfect, autistic storm.

The first full day we were there, Max was already over it. We had just traveled a few weeks before, he was done with people, he was done with wearing clothes, he was just *done*. Every time I tried to take a phone call or do some sort of work, he would meltdown which resulted in me having a meltdown.

News alert: I am human. I get frustrated when things do not play out the way I want them to, I get tired, and I have my limits. That day pushed me over the edge and I ended up walking away from my son, going into the bathroom in our hotel room, and having a good cry. Then I took a deep breath and took a second look at what was on my calendar, evaluated their importance, then proceeded to reschedule all of my calls.

I came out of the bathroom, gave Max a hug, asked what he would like to do, and all he wanted was for me to sit with him. So, I did. After a little while, I told him that I was going to stay there but that I needed to be on the computer for thirty minutes. He set my alarm, and I knocked out all of the things I could that were on my list in those thirty minutes. The alarm went off, I shut it down, quickly rearranged my to-do list for the next day, and snuggled with him.

The past Mel wouldn't have done that. The past Mel would've gotten mad, thought my whole day was ruined, felt like a failure, and then mentally punished myself as I was sitting with my son. Instead of acknowledging as I would now that this is the time/energy I have, these are the priorities I have that fit that, stopping when I'm done, and being present for Max.

We women are such an all-or-nothing community. It's insane! We think by having a plan we're just going to straight-away launch into it, hit the ground running, and everything's just going to come right through, right? And sure, no problem, you'll figure it all out! Yes, you will. But you have to prioritize those steps in order to truly create what you want. Otherwise, it's just going to be this total hodge-podge of noise.

I love that this "system" is customizable. You can structure it or un-structure it as much as you need to or want to. You are a person by design, right? You have a way of doing things by design. We all do. And it's so funny when people write these books that tell you how to do things. They make it sound like, "If you don't apply every single step, then you fail!" Untrue!

Maybe not all of their steps are good for you. But bits and pieces certainly may be. By correlating that to what you want and the time you have, you start customizing your calendar correctly to whatever fits your life.

THE ART OF CUSTOMIZATION

A lot of people get too caught up in the meaning of custom-ization. I've done some research on the word "customize" and the people who've used it in their book titles or sections of their books, and the resounding feedback was, "Well, how can it be customized? We all have different businesses," or "You don't know me so how can it be customized?"

The way I use this term is teaching my clients that their action steps and plan of action are, in fact, "customizable." This means that you can take the pieces you need to work on, and adapt them to the time that you have available by customizing their level of priority on your list. . They're customized to what you want and what you are looking to accomplish.

I've learned that many people get too caught up in systems and rigid regulations. They think it has to be a 1, 2, 3, 4 process with no room for adjustments. All or nothing. And that it has to either fit with their business and rules and their language or it's bullshit.

With my process, I always like to use air quotes around the word "customizable." I'm sure that as you've read this book, there have been some chapters and steps where you've said to yourself, "Nah, I already got that. That doesn't really speak to me." And that's great. But obviously something is missing somewhere along the way, or you wouldn't be reading this book to begin with. Maybe it's identifying what you want, or maybe it is just the boundaries to say "no" to shit that distracts you and pulls you off of your path.

So, I'm challenging you to identify it. What is that missing piece? And if you customize that with the strengths you already have and the process you've already established, it takes you to that next level. It fixes that item on your "not so much" list.

This may sound overly simplistic to you, but I believe the best-customized planning is done once you figure out what to customize, what needs adjusting or tweaking so that your plan works best for you. And that certainly can change over time. Depending on how your day rolls out with some unexpected factors, your plan may wind up changing day to day.

One of the contributing factors as to why you find it difficult to go with the flow more often is that typically, women don't give themselves permission to change.[3] Men traditionally have an easier time of rolling with change and moving forward. Maybe it's built into their DNA? I'm being facetious here, of course. But I know that we women seem to be more geared toward perfectionism and staying the course no matter what, rather than simply allowing ourselves to shift gears, maybe even just slightly, to create the best ultimate outcome in various situations.

It does seem that there's an inherent difference in the approach to change between the masculine/feminine. Personally, looking at the men in my life—my grandfathers, my father—they were all entrepreneurs. If something didn't work, then they pitched it and tried something different or adjusted it and tried again. For some reason, with the women that I've worked with, they try the same thing over and over and over again. That's the epitome of Einstein's definition of insanity:

---

3   Warell, Margie. "Why Women Need to Stop Selling Themselves Short." Harvard Business Review. August 3, 2019. https://www.forbes.com/sites/margiewarrell/2019/08/03/why-women-need-to-stop-selling-themselves-short/#1bd6ed6d70f8

"Doing the same thing over and over and expecting different results."

When my female clients have announced what they're going to roll out/ launch, they feel like it's a failure if they have to shift and/or adjust it. I'm here to say, "Stop beating yourself up and assuming you're a failure. Just customize your approach!" Use the knowledge you now have, remember what you want, reanalyze the time you have available and reboot.

There is research that shows how women all too often abandon their dreams instead of figuring out a different approach.[4] If you feel this applies to you, I'm here to tell you there is hope.

First, sit down for a few minutes, take some deep breaths, and release any and all negative thoughts you've been having about your current situation. Then have a good talk with yourself, saying something like, "No, this goal is a good one. I'm not going to walk away from it and give up. Now it's simply a matter of allowing myself to be open to figuring out how to go about it differently to get what I want."

Encouragingly talking to yourself to keep your chin up is really powerful. You might find that having such self-pep talks in the mirror works well for you. I sometimes talk to Max's goldfish. Whatever your method, please know that there are

---

4   Gourani, Soulaima. "Why Most Women Give Up On Their Dreams." Forbes. July 29, 2019. https://www.forbes.com/sites/soulaimagourani/2019/07/29/why-most-women-give-up-on-their-dreams/#4ef728df2082

always things you can change and do differently to keep moving forward.

You, your goals, your business are all non-negotiables. Nobody else is going to do this for you. So again, going back to previous chapters, when you need to customize your calendar, you go back to square one; sit and review your strengths, your "not so muches." And back to that classic bottom line of, "What do I want? How do I want to spend my time? What's my energy like right now?"

So that's more insight into what I mean when I say "customizable." It amounts to being ready to have a good solid self-talk when it's necessary to support the energy, strengths and goals that you have on that given day, minute, moment, or decision.

You can take it a step further as you're customizing your daily situation, by taking that breather and recentering yourself. Then you're in a better position to take a look at your weekly and monthly goals.

Figure out how to flex to your strengths and advocate for your weaknesses.

It's so valuable to understand that when you do this, you're stretching, adapting, and, at the same time, strengthening your skills.

This process reminds me of the bamboo tree. They are able to bend so agilely and, because of that, they are incredibly strong.[5] In fact, even though bamboo is so lightweight, it's been proven to be three times as strong as timber and has a greater tensile strength than steel when it's used in building. It even withstands compression better than one of the hardest building materials in the world—concrete! Chinese bamboo trees[6] don't grow during their first five years.

The ground must be watered and fertilized consistently during this time. And then, whoa! Once they break the ground, they shoot up to ninety feet or so, sometimes growing rapidly on a daily basis. This happens because someone has lovingly nurtured them before they are even visible, just like I'm encouraging you to be patient and nurture yourself.

Be bamboo and know that the more flexible you can learn to be, the stronger you can become. Your ultimate goal is to have this strength that is able to bend and flex and rise to opportunities. Even though it's hard to understand, by doing so, it will help you begin to grasp the concept of, "Sometimes you need to slow down in order to speed up."

The problem with our microwave society is that everyone has gotten spoiled and always wants instant gratification. The

5   Forever Bamboo. "Bamboo Poles - Stronger Than You Think." Foreverbamboo.com. Accessed June 14, 2020. https://www.foreverbamboo.com/blog/bamboo-poles-stronger-than-you-think/#:~:-text=How%20Strong%20is%20Bamboo%3F,-Bamboo%20can%20easily&text=Bamboo%20is%20a%20very%20light,or%20stretching%20pressure%20before%20breaking.
6   Goalcast.com. "Les Brown: How Bamboo Trees Will Bring Out Your Best Self." Goalcast.com. July 10, 2018. https://www.goalcast.com/2018/07/10/les-brown-how-bamboo-trees-will-bring-out-your-best-self

idea of slowing down to speed up is definitely a paradox. It is particularly true for women to understand how important that is for them, because we are the ultimate multi-taskers, aren't we? Many women simultaneously juggle their careers with their family, partner/spouse, friends, pets, and more. I want to encourage you to take the time to breathe and slow down now and again. It really helps.

Remember to take excellent care of yourself first, for, after all, *you* are the most profitable avenue.

TRY THIS

You may have noticed that the thread running through this chapter is this idea of giving yourself permission to move on. There are various ways to achieve this. If you're a kinesthetic person/learning, here's a tip you might find useful.

Draw an imaginary line (or lay down a paper one if you prefer) on the floor. Stand on one side, take a breath, and as you exhale, step over the line and don't go back. This helps instill muscle memory along with your brain's memory capacity and strongly confirms for you that you have left the problem behind and are moving forward.

When we do something physically to reinforce a point or decision, it can be very empowering. Obviously, you could write the problem down, burn it, or tear it up. But it's useful to have some type of physical ceremony that will help you move forward so you can let it go.

If you consider yourself to be spiritual or more metaphysically inclined, by all means, meditate on it, or go for that good burning and releasing ceremony.

If you're into the cycles of the moon or astrological shifts and want to align such activities with that, go for it. If you're more on what most people would call the "practical" side, just make sure you take that moment of just sitting with it for five deep breaths, all the way in and out.

Allow yourself to feel the emotion—be pissed, be sad, or upset. Do whatever you need to do to recognize that feeling. But don't stay there. Your next step is to ask yourself, "Okay. Now what can I control?" Well, the first thing is how you choose to react. And then what to do afterward with that reaction. Then you just reapply that to whatever mood you're in.

If this is an extremely emotional situation, then you reapply the priority that *you are first*. You are your best asset on all levels. If you realize that you need to take a break and focus on taking care of you in order to come back tomorrow a little bit better, do that. Give yourself permission to recharge and refresh your energy, lift your mood.

Tomorrow you'll come back stronger. Maybe not 100%, or maybe you will be; the important thing is to find your best catharsis and employ it. You might get the clarity that what you're doing gives you a hint of, "This isn't the right step."

This is not a step back, mind you. It's taking a step to decide and doing a quick evaluation: "Now, what do I want?

What is the time that I have? What is that intention, and what can I start applying to get me connected not only to myself but to my business, my clients and moving forward?"

By the way, you'll always be customizing. You're going to continually be readjusting because you're learning and growing all the time.

JUDY'S STORY

This plan helps you to create a "structure" around your day, not a routine. People get caught up in routines and typically lose that important connection to what they want.

This was a fear of Judy's.

During one of our sessions, she asked me if she will be working her day, the same, every day, forever. To which I responded, "Nope, not unless you are done growing yourself and your business."

A routine just means you have to be consistent. So, what is that consistency in? And how can you customize a plan or a week that keeps you engaged, keeps you connected, and keeps you consistent? That's a routine.

Then she asked, "But what if I don't want to do this?"

To which I responded, "Then recognize what you do want, reanalyze the priorities that you have that are aligned with what you want now, reapply and move on!"

And she let out the biggest sigh of relief I have ever heard.

She was suffering from what I like to call "Corporate PTSD." She was a recruiter in the corporate space for twenty-five years. She had started her business about six months prior to working with me and, financially, she was CRUSHING it; but mentally and emotionally she was struggling.

"What if I don't want to be a recruiter? Maybe that's just all I know," she said.

I told her, "Okay. But guess what? You own your own business. You can make this whatever you want it to be. Maybe recruiting has been that first level and from there you could turn into a mentor, a speaker, or maybe you just say 'fuck it' and you open up an office in Africa. I don't know. But that's the joy of always checking in. You have always full say."

If you have any type of anxiety or fear about doing the same thing over and over again, then don't!

Judy has a true gift for recruiting, so she decided to stick with it; however, she is now excited about what that can evolve into and what her next level will be!

When you think about it, there is so much latitude in the "customization" space. It's virtually an "anything is possible" feeling to know that you have the space to adjust in small ways or big ways; you can create these amazing shifts that are always lined with what you want. So give yourself permission and to do it powerfully!

My goal behind *She Profits* is to empower you to know that YOU profit. That's your goal: profit, profit, profit—but it's not just about money. I mean profit and grow abundant in every aspect of your life including mental, emotional and financial profit.

I want to make sure that you understand that there are layers to this, having this mindset of profitability. That it's larger than just money, and that checking in and getting control of customizing your life on a daily, weekly, monthly, and even yearly basis makes a ton of difference. Anything you do has an impact. A lot of people would think, "Oh, well, but you're telling me if I take a day off, that actually floats to my bottom line in a positive way." "Yes, it does!" It's counter-intuitive, but it's true.

This also has to do with sustainability. I mean, face it: Nobody started their own business to be a miserable cow. We start our own business because we want to create what-ever *we* define as what we want, whether it's a comfortable little business or an empire. Why simply sustain your lifestyle when you can enhance it greatly? It's up to you. You're just utilizing one profit avenue so that you can strengthen the other one. Looking at it, that's why *The 4-Hour Work Week* is so fuckin' sexy!

Still, that author doesn't explain it in the same way that I do, and that's OK. I'm all about teaching you powerful pieces about giving yourself permission and seeing that whatever you do—as long as it attaches to you, your passion and what you believe in—will have a positive physical outcome.

RECAP

- "Customize" your day by aligning the prioritized tasks you have with the energy and time you have every day.

- When things shoot to shit—recognize, reanalyze, reapply and MOVE ON!

- You will never do the same thing every day until you die unless you have decided to stop growing yourself and your business.

- Give yourself permission and do it powerfully!

ACTION STEPS

- Let's practice how to "Be:"

  ○ Sit down, close your eyes and take three deep breaths.

  ○ Either out loud or inside your head, say something positive about your day. Examples:

    – "I am going to get this done."

    – "I am a badass woman who is on a mission!"

    – "This, too, shall pass; now open your eyes and conquer your day!"

  ○ Slowly open your eyes and take a look at your day with a new set of eyes.

CHAPTER 6

STEP #5:
PUT. THIS.
INTO.
ACTION!!

I'LL LET YOU IN on a little secret. When I give talks, I usually lead up to this point with no warning that we're about to cover the last step in my methodology. I hide that slide from them. I kind of make a big deal out of it by announcing, "Hold onto your hat—here comes the pièce de ré·sis·tance." But in a book, it's a wee bit different, I've discovered.

Nonetheless, here comes that golden nugget of final wisdom that I have to share with you for now, and it's what separates the women who are successful from the women who are in the same space—mentally, emotionally and financially—months, maybe years, after I have met them.

"Give it to me Mel! What is that magic?"

It's so simple you're going to be blown away, and I can sum it up in one succinct word:

ACTION.

I know you're thinking, "Well, that was a bit anticlimactic, of course this is the last step."

Hashtag fact. However, I have seen this time and time again with the women I am working with and speaking to. They plan EVERYTHING, then plan how to execute that plan, and then plan on what they need to execute that plan…

We're students of personal development and we fuckin' love being on that merry-go-round, don't we? We can readily quote Jim Rohn, Susan Powter, John Maxwell, Suze Orman, Darren Hardy and Tony Robbins out the wazoo. We know their books inside and out, and we loved reading and/or listening to them. But you know the crazy part about that? Most of us are still stuck in the same spot quoting those things because we are not actually implementing what we learned from them.

Most of that obstacle comes from the fact that we are too overwhelmed with what to implement because we feel like we need to do it all at once! Another thought is that since the entire plan doesn't "fit" with their end goal, they think, "Well, I don't need this whole plan, so guess it's not for me." STOP!

There are gems in all systems, this book included, you just need to customize what parts you put into action first that will continue that momentum.

Going back to my background in fitness, I would have clients say things to me like, "I want to quit smoking, quit drinking, eat healthy and work out five times a week." Fantastic. But you can't do all of that at once. You literally can't. Your body's going to say, "Fuck you!"

So, what can you do to not only build your confidence and your consistency that will give you the energy and motivation to then keep on building? What is that one thing, that one priority? It will leap out at you if you give it the chance. And when it does, start putting it into action.

Remember, it can be something little to start with, such as, "I'm going to start with waking up at 6 a.m." Brilliant! You just created more time for yourself. Woot woot! After you do that, what's the next thing that you want to incorporate into your routine or your plan in order to create what you want?

And the process continues from there. But it's that first actionable step that is so blatantly important, so don't skip it!

LILY'S STORY

Lily's story is one of the most perfect examples of how profitable utilizing this plan is.

She's a travel agent at her own VIP travel agency and part of her offering is that she can not only plan your trip but she also takes small groups on these amazing excursions. So, she plans everything out but she's also your tour guide and travels with you. How awesome is that?!

Here's the part of her story I want to share with you. She came to me at the beginning of summer and she was freaking out because she realized that she could only work a total of six weeks over the next three months because she booked so many travel tours.

She panicked. "How am I going to make this work? I'm going to Scotland, going to Iceland, I'm going to the U.K.— what have I done to myself? Somehow during all this traveling, I still have to build a business!"

The first thing I did to help her was to say, "Okay. Just stop for a minute. What do you want to make every month just to keep you afloat?" We all have times in our lives when we have to do just the bare minimum to get by. So again, my question was, "What do you need to stay afloat?" That removed all of the emotions from it and put her quandary in terms of pure facts.

She figured out that she needed to close six new clients (two per month) just to stay afloat. So, the next step I coached her with was, "Great! Okay, now let's look at the resources that you already have. How many people do you have in the funnel? How many people can you close early? What does that look like?"

We got her available resources completely mapped out: how many people did she need to fill that hopper? How many people did she need to reach out to in order to get that done?

Then, to tame her time, we made a calendar that showed only the days that she could work. That way she didn't look at the calendar thinking, "Fuck! I can't work these three weeks." Instead, she could look at this calendar a different way and say, "Okay. Today's June 2nd – I can work today!"

We planned action.

Now I'm going to be honest and report that she did not close the six clients she wanted, she booked TEN and also came back from her last trip with six profitable leads. This turned into her highest profitable months ever in her business!!! All of that happened because she put our plan into action.

Once she got present and focused, it became a win-win. All because she was able to take away that fear of, "I can't work during this time" and replaced it with, "I can work on these days, so what do I want? What do I need to do to get there in the time that I have?" Then prioritized day by day.

YOUR STORY

I don't know your story, but I know that the ones I shared of myself and my amazing clients/colleagues have resonated with you. I know that, just like all of us, you are still writing your story.

Here's an interesting fact I've picked up by working with clients: Entrepreneurship affects everybody in the same way. It doesn't matter how old you are when you become an entrepreneur. You're still going to find these interesting hurdles that will get recognized and resolved by utilizing one of these points. I work with women who are in their 20s all the way to their mid 50s; some who have never had a "real job" and others who have been in corporations for twenty years or more. Their common struggle starts from the same place: overwhelm created by everything they think they need to do to be successful.

Some have become empty-nesters and it suddenly hits them that they have more say on what they want to create but have no idea what they want because they have always put everyone else first.

Others are struggling with what I call "corporate PTSD" when it hits them, "Wait a minute. I don't have a name behind me. I didn't realize how much work this was. I didn't realize the processes that were involved. I just kind of expected to magically cross over into this new way of working."

When a client tells me they're in that state of overwhelm and doubt, that's when I have a lot of "Come to Jesus talks" when I tell them, "We need to talk about this because it is affecting your business. You can't just sweep it under the rug. It's going to bite you in the ass. So, let's identify the pieces that are freaking you out. What are the pieces that are stopping you?"

Then I take it a step further by asking, "What if things aren't working because it's what you thought you needed to do to be successful? Sure, you had success in this category while you were a cog in the corporate machine, but now this is just you. Do you really still want to work in the same capacity, or would you rather tackle something totally different and apply the skills you've built to that?"

It always comes down to those internal obstacles that hit at a certain degree at different times. We all hit them. Here's a secret that you probably already know—they never really stop. But having that constant connection with yourself and that regular check-in of, "What do I want?" helps you bypass the obstacle or challenge faster because you recognize it. Again, once you've recognized it, either you've blessed and released it, or you've given it gratitude and moved on. Recognize, reapply, and move on!

My goal for you is that you implement the tips and tools I'm sharing that work for you, so that it all supports you in living your best, most beautiful life. That is where the phrase "She Profits" is applicable: you will be profitable mentally, emotionally, and financially every damn day. A profitability that is sustainable, rewarding, and 100% yours.

For any reason if you choose not to do anything else with this book, I encourage you to share it with someone you feel will make use of it. There's so much power in paying things forward in life.

I've learned the hard way that, as women, sometimes we just need to take a breath and tell ourselves, "Shut the hell up!" when we start to beat ourselves up, such as complaining about, "I'm doing the same thing over and over and not seeing results." Did you know that is the definition of Insanity?

It's OK.

Get out of that pattern ASAP and move forward. Shift to a different conversation. Remember, you have full say. Even if you think, "I don't have a choice;" well, yeah, you do. You're the one who just chose to say you don't have a choice! Nobody's forcing you to say or think that.

Even that little step making a quick mind-flip: reframing or reapplying. Customizing when it hits you, "Ok that self-talk ain't helping nobody, now can I flip this?" And it's those little things you do every day that make the biggest difference.

Are you trying to tame your time, but someone is trying to insert themselves into your space? You have full say to tell them "fuck off," but nicely. It's very easy to do, I do it all the time.

Customize your life and pay attention to that all the time, and how powerful that can be. You owe it to yourself to customize your life because there are so many women who make themselves smaller to make others bigger, and that's not a necessity. Stand up for yourself, honor your time commitment, and don't let anyone else take that away from you! Know that advocating for yourself is definitely a way to be the best you can be, which will inspire other people to do the same.

PROLOGUE PEP TALK

OK, let's do a full recap of everything we worked on in this book.

Step #1- Identify 'What do *I* want?'
Step #2- Tame your time (You have FULL SAY on how you spend the time that you have!)
Step #3- Prioritize your tasks according to what you want.
Step #4- Customize!
Step #5- *ACTION!!!*

Now although I have thrown a lot at you in a very short amount of time, my hope is that you have taken your time with each step. But do not get discouraged if you are totally motivated to create what you want but are overwhelmed with knowing where to start.

Remember, this is SIMPLE and CUSTOMIZABLE, so let's walk through this step by step.

Look through your notes/highlights, however you have been keeping track of what created your OHF moments. Now write down the ones that answer this question: "What do I want to start applying from this book first?" Congratulations, you have just identified what you want!!

It can be as small as "I am going to turn off my notifications and only check my social media twice a day." Remember, it's the little things you do, every day, that make the biggest difference.

Let's move on…where are you going to fit this into your day/week?

Shit went south on that day? Customize and reprioritize!

Don't Do This Alone.

When I work with people, something that they often tell me is, "The thing that helped me most about working with you is that you held me accountable." If that's the case, then it's pretty clear that most of us would benefit greatly by having some kind of ongoing accountability partner. For entrepreneurs, doing so can help you avoid the whole illusion of, "I'm out here all on my own on this lonely island. No wonder I'm not a success."

Trust me, I know that can be a lonely undertaking. I'm far from saying that it isn't. Yes, I'm blessed to have a family of entrepreneurs and I have built a great circle of friends who are amazing entrepreneurs, so I'm fortunate to have my own little built-in council of support. But I have found that the reason a lot of people hire me is that they don't know how to go about creating a support system.

You may have great friends who you love to death, but they can't understand this life that you have chosen, so their support helps you get only so far. You get that quick pat on your head like you're a little kid while saying, "Oh, that's such a great idea." But then no support to help you create action steps, so you don't take any and therefore get no results.

Sometimes they reach out to me because they find themselves in a completely new world and feel lost. They have no idea how to put into action their desire, their plan, or business. They want to, but they don't have the tools or the support system to turn to. In other words, they just really have no clue how to function in this new world.

If you're there, don't despair! There are ways to create that much needed support and mentorship.

You can create accountability partners via social media. For instance, reach out to your contacts with a message that says, "Hey, Jill. Long time no talk. Listen, I'm starting a new venture and looking to build a supportive network and you were the first person who popped in my head! How about a virtual coffee sometime to catch up?"

Same thing for all the other platforms, and very quickly you can find your tribe!

Certainly, "live" networking provides a big bonus in connecting with like-minded people in a room that's electrically charged with excitement. That in itself is just an awesome place for people. You look around, smile, and your heart sings as you realize, "I'm not alone!"

Or it can be virtual, especially in the aftermath of the COVID-19 quarantine. I'm hearing a lot of people say now that, "Who would have thought that I could build strong relationships virtually?" Well, those of us who have been building them virtually for a long time know that you can do that, and it works. But because of the pandemic, people's newfound awareness of the value of a virtual coffee or lunch meeting is huge.

I could write a whole other book on the power of networking, but I know you have enough on your plate right now. When you are ready, check out my website link that is at the end of this book, I have a ton of resources on there that will help you prioritize that next avenue.

This isn't "good-bye," this is "see you soon!"

Now that we have met, I am going to tell you what I tell everyone who I have had the privilege of sharing time, space, and energy with: I am here to support you 100%.

P.S. I'm not the type of coach that just gives you all of this and leaves you to your own devices. I have an amazing community you can join to continue to support you as you create, implement, and live your profitable life. Head over to my website, www.melmcsherry.com, to learn how to join.

Have questions? Email me : support@melmcsherry.com

Want more of me? Follow me on Instagram: @mel_mcsherry

Always in your corner, Mel.

ACKNOWLEDGEMENTS

THERE IS NO "I" in team and there is no way on this earth I could have created this book without mine!

First, I would like to thank my father for being my lifelong example and inspiration. For showing me what the life of an entrepreneur, parent, and partner is as you create what you want, as well as supporting me as I designed my own entrepreneurial path.

Next, I would like to thank my clients for trusting me and allowing me to be a part of their journey. Every day I learn something from them and I am so grateful and honored to share space with them!

I would also like to thank Melissa G. Wilson, my book-creation coach, and her team at Networlding Publishing, as well as my right-hand woman, Loni Nelson, and her team for their unwavering support, patience, excitement, and tenacity. Without you, this book would be nothing but a file on my computer and a goal written on a board. Thank you for making this become a reality and a success!

Finally, to my son Max. You have taught me more than anyone about my strengths as well as my not-so-much areas. Your unconditional love has helped me through some tough times and your high-fives are my favorite way to celebrate my successes. My hope is that, no matter what you create in your life, it is always 100% yours. I love you!

APPENDIX

Step #1– Identify:

- What you want in your business—not what you think you CAN achieve, but what you WANT to achieve.
- Who can support you to get what you want?
- Who you need to be to get what you want?
- Who do you want to work with?

Step #2 – Tame your time.

- Control the time that you have.
- Create boundaries around that time.
- Identify how you are stealing from yourself in Time and Money.

Step #3– Prioritize your tasks.

- Understand the importance of knowing what is on your to-do list and why it's on there.
- It's possible to feel successful every day, no matter how much time you have.

Step #4- Customize your calendar.

- "Customize" your day by aligning the prioritized tasks you have with the energy and time you have every day.
- When things shoot to shit recognize, reanalyze, reapply and MOVE ON!
- You will never do the same thing every day until you die unless you have decided to stop growing yourself as well as your business.
- Give yourself permission and do it powerfully!

Step #5- ACTION!!!

BONUS RESOURCE PDF

https://www.melmcsherry.com/Book-Bonus